# Blessings in Disguise

Maranatha Conference

Compiled by

Living Parables of Central Florida

# Blessings in Disguise

## Volume 4

Copyright © 2019 Living Parables of Central Florida, Inc.

All rights reserved.

ISBN: 978-1-945976-68-1

Published by EA Books Publishing a division of
Living Parables of Central Florida, Inc. a 501c3
EABooksPublishing.com

Living Parables of Central Florida, a 501c3

Living Parables of Central Florida Living Parables of Central Florida, Inc., of which EABooks Publishing is a division, offers publishing contests at Christian conferences to provide opportunities for unpublished authors to be discovered and earn publishing credits. We publish high quality, self-published books that bring glory and honor to God's Kingdom.

Blessings often come disguised in hard times, difficult circumstances, broken relationships, or shattered dreams. Sometimes the blessings are unexpected hugs from God. The Bible promises us that He will turn all things for good for those who love the Lord. This is the hope believers cling to when the storm clouds gather and when the rain is so hard, we can't see the next step. May you hear the hope these stories bring and are encouraged to look for your own blessings in disguise.

# ACKNOWLEDGMENTS

We'd like to thank the director of our conferences, Sherry Hoppen, for encouraging and equipping writers and speakers for the glory of the Kingdom of God. We wish to thank Cheri Cowell and her wonderful team at EABooks Publishing for giving us this opportunity. We thank our many friends and family for supporting us in our writing dreams. And most importantly, we want to thank our Lord and Savior Jesus Christ for His gifts—may this book bring you the honor and glory you deserve.

# TABLE OF CONTENTS

| | |
|---|---|
| Acknowledgements | iv |
| Unemployed Blessings<br>*Nancy Elizabeth Lynn* | 1 |
| Hope for Today and Tomorrow<br>*Renee Joy Janzen* | 5 |
| Freedom Through Trials<br>*Sofia Tjiptadjaja* | 9 |
| CVS Coupon Couple<br>*Grace S. Johnson* | 13 |
| Crossroad Moments – Choosing Faith Over Fear<br>*Karen L. Wisniewski* | 17 |
| A Journey Interrupted<br>*Juanita Copley* | 21 |
| Missed Bus<br>*Alicia Herrington* | 25 |
| A Son's Sacrifice – A Father's Redemption<br>*Dawn M. Durkee* | 29 |
| This is the Greatest Show<br>*Cindi Raymond* | 33 |
| Serendipity and Me!<br>*Carol E. Veenstra* | 37 |

Expectations with Elizabeth and Mary 41
*Phyllis Wynsma*

He Stayed On the Cross 45
*Kimberly J. Price*

The Asia Experiment 47
*Tracy Herrington*

# Blessings in Disguise

# Unemployed Blessings

*Nancy Elizabeth Lynn*

Cassie was sitting on the ground in the back yard plucking at a blade of grass. Anna approached her quietly and sat down nearby. "I don't want things to change," Cassie said without looking up. "I don't want to go home where everything will be different. It feels awful and it's not fair."

"I understand," was Anna's response. "It's difficult to see the good in something that feels so tragic. It's happened to me a couple of times and I still remember the pain of it."

"When did it happen to you?" Cassie asked not being able to completely hide her fourteen year old curiosity.

"I was a single parent while my daughters were growing up," Anna began. "I didn't have a family that I could turn to for help and I felt completely responsible for my daughters' well-being with no one to fall back on if something went wrong. Most of my daughters' childhood I worked two jobs or else was working full time and going to college full time working toward a degree that I hoped would insure that I would never be unemployed. I was terrified of not having an income and being able to provide for my children. But even with all my hard work and good intentions the worst still happened and I found myself out of work.

I had always worked for small businesses doing accounting. More than once the owners of the business that I worked for ended up selling the company or moving the business out of town and I was forced to find a new place to work. I always found another job quickly but it would be for another small business and after a few years the same thing would happen. Once I completed my degree, and found myself again looking for a new job because my employer was moving his office to another city, I decided rather than taking an accounting job at another small business I would take a job with a local CPA firm. I thought that because the CPA firm was owned by multiple people and had existed in town for many years, it was less likely that it would go out of business or move out of town so I would be able to stay with this company until I was able to retire.

I actually did work there for eight and a half years and I enjoyed many of the clients that I was assigned to, but I never felt like I had the support of the partners. Many of them were unkind. When there was a problem with one of my clients the partners at this firm didn't hesitate to make me the scapegoat. The client had no problem with me and was very quick to tell me so, but the CPA firm needed a fall guy.

I was absolutely mortified the day they walked me out of the building like I was a criminal. They wouldn't even let me go back to my desk and get my things. I went home in intense emotional and physical pain. I curled up on the bed that night praying that I wouldn't wake up the next day. I wasn't suicidal. I had no desire to die. I was just tired of working so hard and having none of it matter. I laid on my bed trying not to think about my kids or my grandkids because I knew I really did want to wake up the next day. I just didn't want to deal

with that kind of pain and rejection any more. At that point everything seemed very, very hopeless."

"I know that feeling," Cassie inserted glumly.

"Well, the next day did come," Anna continued. "I looked into unemployment compensation and updated my resume and prepared to do whatever I had to do to get another job. What other choice did I have? But before I was able to pursue this, I received a phone call from one of my clients who asked me to come to work for them as a contracted accountant. By working for them directly, rather than through the CPA firm, they could pay me more than the CPA firm had paid me and yet less than they had been paying the CPA firm for my work. They knew all about the reasons I was fired and knew that my other client hadn't had any issue with me at all. I had also been working with them through the CPA firm for years so they knew my work. They helped me set up my own business and they were fine with my taking on other clients.

So that's what I did. I started my own business, took on other clients, made more money and had much more flexibility in my schedule than I had ever had before. I've been working that way ever since.

To this day, I am amazed at how quickly things can turn around and how a real, genuine blessing can come out of something so painful. I never would have set out on my own if that CPA firm hadn't been so awful to me."

"Honestly, Cassie," Anna said touching her shoulder causing Cassie to look up into her face. "To this day I remember how painful that experience was for me. I still think those former employers were very unkind in the way they handled things. But they did me one of the biggest favors of my life. The good that came out of that very awful situation was something I will always be grateful for."

"I realize things don't usually turn around in forty-eight hours. But I think having good things come out of very difficult situations happens more often than we realize."

At this Cassie only shrugged. She wasn't completely buying what Anna was telling her but at least she was being open to the possibility.

"Since there is nothing you can do to change your situation," Anna concluded, "maybe the best course of action is to 'accept what you cannot change' and watch for the blessings that might come out of it. It may take a little time but I'm betting you will find that you enjoy your life even in spite of the changes. It will still be a very good life."

Nancy Elizabeth Lynn is a self-employed accountant who enjoys gardening, walking and writing stories. I single parented my two daughters who are now married and have given me three grandchildren. I travel between Massachusetts and Michigan to spend time with them.

Even as a child, I made up stories. I began writing again once my children were grown.

# Hope for Today and Tomorrow

*Renee Joy Janzen*

**TRUTH: His Words and His Promises**

*Therefore, let those also who suffer according to the will of God entrust their souls to a faithful Creator in doing what is right* (1 Peter 4:19).

**TRUTH: In Real Life**

Did she take the wrong train? Nothing looked familiar to Eva. Her life was not as she had imagined. Decades ago when Eva had stood at the altar and said, "I do", her vision was a home filled with happy, healthy children. Instead, she watched in helpless agony as her precious little ones suffered daily from a rare and incurable disease. Now, the unthinkable was happening. The most joyful and delightful of her babes lay beside her only moments from death. As she sat holding her child's hand, watching the little chest rise and fall with each shallow and labored breath, Eva could sense herself sliding into hopelessness. Had all her prayers gone unheard? How could a loving God take her child from her? Then it happened. Even as she asked the questions, an overwhelming holiness filled the room. It enveloped Eva causing her words to be uttered in reverent whispers. Effortlessly, her foreboding was transformed to quieting peace. Her doubts were changed by a soothing and safe love. She was being firmly held by loving hands. She was being carried safely with strong and sturdy arms. In that moment, John 12:27, came clearly to her mind.

During the last week of His life on earth, and knowing His suffering and death was near, Jesus said, "Now my soul has become troubled; and what shall I say, 'Father, save Me from this hour'? But for this purpose I came to this hour. Father, glorify Thy name." There, by her much-loved child's bed, Eva experienced a quiet understanding. In the midst of tragedy, she was not to ask, "Why?", or "What did I do to deserve this?", or even "Save me from this trouble!" Rather, Eva's response was: For this purpose I came. This is the reason I am here. Father, how can I glorify You in the midst of sickness and death? When her child passed from this life to the next, Eva watched in a hollowed awe. She understood life was in the midst of death. It was not the end; it was the beginning. No, Eva's life did not look as she had expected; rather, it was richer, deeper, and more beautiful than she could have ever imagined. What an incredible honor to help a child transition to heaven into the arms of an everlasting Father.

**My Prayer:**

You tell me straight up that I will have many troubles in this life. Help me discern if my current suffering is the result of my living according to Your will. Silence my righteous pride. Silence the accuser within. Let me hear only Your voice. Then give me strength to do what is right even when it is unpopular, even when it is politically incorrect, even when no one else is doing it. This day, I entrust my soul to You, my faithful Creator.

**Laying It Down Questions for Reflection and Discussion:**

How have you suffered in the past? Where was God during your suffering? If you are unable to answer that question, close your eyes and ask Him to show you.

Renee Joy Janzen was raised in Indiana and spent much of her adult life as an attorney and educator in Oklahoma. Currently, she spends her time in her passionate interests of writing, hiking and cycling throughout America. She breaks/brakes regularly for her greatest passion of spending time with her children and grandchildren.

# Freedom Through Trials

*Sofia Tjiptadjaja*

*"I have told you these things, so that in me you may have peace. In this world you will have trouble. But take heart! I have overcome the world."*
(John 16:33)

My naïve younger self used to think I can outsmart suffering. In my youthful arrogance, I thought if I were diligent at school, worked hard, got myself a solid husband, raised good kids and did not allow our family anywhere close to worldly vices such as gambling, pornography or drugs, then I would pretty much be able to cruise through this life, avoiding much of its suffering. This was my grand life plan.

Little did I know suffering would knock on each of our doors sooner or later. There is no exception, it will come to everybody's life, the good people and the bad people. We all will have to face suffering in this life. If it is knocking at your door today, it will surely knock at my door tomorrow. Suffering will come upon us uninvited, it will barge in and bring pain into our lives. The pain can be physical pains causing different degrees of disabilities. Or it can be emotional pains in varied forms of heart maladies. Or it can be the spiritual pain of being disconnected with God. Most likely, it will be a nuanced combination of physical, emotional and spiritual pains.

Suffering can invade our lives in a pompous and catastrophic fashion, like in the death of loved ones, financial crisis or betrayals. Though more often, suffering creeps in chronically into our lives, like in the bad habits, sickness and addictions that left us hopeless and defeated, in the unmet expectations that make us feel unloved, or in the daily grinds of life that make us weary. We have little control over its coming and going, it stays and gnaws at our sense of well-being.

When my husband chose to leave a comfortable job and explore the rugged terrain of entrepreneurship a few years ago, I couldn't help thinking we were being foolish. We entered a 'suffering state' on our own account, abandoning steady good income for so many uncertainties. My husband was adamant with his decisions and I was resentful towards him because I thought he was dragging the whole family to 'suffer' for his personal ambition.

Yet God is sovereign, He is good and all-knowing. God really knows what is best for us more than we do. In hindsight, I realized my husband was being sincere with his faith and trying his best to follow the call he felt coming from God. My husband has stretched and grown so much as a person because of the challenges he had to face in his business.

I also understand now how much my heart needed major surgery and healing through these financial trials by fire. This could only happen through my own tears and pain, not from inspirations and ideas from books. I can only be amazed at God as the master craftsman. He weaves our decisions and our painful experiences into a customized sanctification process so that our heart can be molded and modeled into one of His masterpieces and become a beautiful offering to Him.

I read an apt quote the other day: "**Adversity** uncovers the essence of a person, while **Prosperity** hides a person's sins." Little did I know God's plan for me was to expose the idols that had hidden in my heart. I was not even fully aware of their presence until the circumstances of life pressed on me and forced my idols to come out of hiding. Dr. Ernie Baker fittingly described that we are like tea bags, everything is latent inside, the hot water only draws out the flavor.

My sense of well-being was under assault; the control and comfort idols inside my heart reared their ugly heads and threw tantrums because I couldn't meet their demands in our current financial circumstances.

I wasn't aware how these idols had kept me in bondage. They had become my ultimate support system, my source of strength and guidance in making life decisions. They had provided visions and illusions of life for me to strive for and I wanted to satisfy them by all means possible. When I could no longer appease them, it caused me so much distress.

I was left with no option. If I wanted to continue to live life peacefully, I would need to cut the chains off of them. It was much easier said than done, these idols had been everything to me. I was frantically grappling to find a new 'rock' to hold on to. Keep in mind, I had been a serious Christian for many years up to that point, I had sufficient theological knowledge to know and believe God is the real Rock and security of life. I will never truly know what my true convictions are until they're tested. My head really knew and believed that fact, but apparently, my heart hadn't jumped ships and changed its allegiance.

God's strategy was to reveal first how truly unreliable this ship I was on, it was a sinking ship. I was obliviously partying on that ship, thinking this ship will carry me to my desired destination. God showed not only it would not carry me to the right destination, but my whole family could be drowned in the journey by living in self-indulgence, keeping us in perpetual 'search and strive' mode but never arriving. My perceived sense of control in life was an utter illusion and the comfort I'd enjoyed did not bring out the best in me.

God wanted to cut me off from my idols and connect to Him in a much deeper way so He alone will be my source of strength, comfort, hope and help. I slowly shifted my gaze from my idols to God and my vision started to change. God gently told me to chart a new course to a better destination He has prepared for me. This new destination might not be glowing and glistening with worldly glitters, but the ultimate beauty will be uncovered in the world to come and it will surpass the other one.

*"I consider that our present sufferings are not worth comparing with the glory that will be revealed in us."*
(Romans 8:18)

Sofia Tjiptadjaja lives in Indonesia, a wife of a wonderful husband and a mother of two tween girls. Her passion is to encourage women to attain a Biblical vision of wholesomeness the way God uniquely designs each woman. Her writings and free e-book Discipleship for Women are available at www.wholesomewomen.org.

# CVS Coupon Couple

*Grace S. Johnson*

One Sunday morning after an argument with my husband, I drove to the local diner to soothe my soul with comfort food. I then justified my decision not to meet him at church by telling myself "We didn't resolve our financial disagreement, so why attend church, put on a happy smile, and pretend all is well with us . . . especially since others use Sunday morning to run errands before their work week?"

After my breakfast, I found a crinkled coupon tucked in my car dash board and decided to make the effort to use it, espccially since CVS was across the street. If you are a CVS customer like myself, most likely their coupons or discounts have become a drawing card to entice you to choose to shop within their walls.

While in CVS purchasing makeup and a toiletry item I really needed, my eye caught a family in the shampoo aisle. Their ethnicity was different from mine, yet I knew instinctively we shared a common bond . . . they too were using "coupons" to gather their wares. Everyone likes to save a little, right?

I pretended not to notice the husband and wife and two elementary aged daughters, but hung close to observe the father holding a three-inch binder full of plastic sleeves. Without trying to stare, I noticed these pages held pockets of well-organized coupons.

The wife held up a shampoo bottle. "Honey, Pantene Pro-V 12 oz. is on sale for $4.99. What coupon do you have for Pantene?"

"Fifty cents off all Pantene products," the husband responded.

During this tender dialogue between this couple over shampoo, I watched the daughters attentively listening and watching their parents. I also thought of the argument over finances my husband and I had just had at home.

So as not to linger too long, I went around the corner but wanted to return to observe this couple more closely. I did, and saw the wife pick up makeup while her amazing interaction with her husband continued.

"Honey, my Maybelline Great Lash Mascara is now $6.99 and if we buy two we get $5 extra buck rewards."

Her husband dug into his large well-organized notebook and pulled up a coupon to match her item. Together they discussed her desired mascara purchase.

"What husband goes to buy shampoo and makeup with his wife, much less care if she is saving cents or dollars on her purchase?" I said to myself.

Again trying to distract myself from this family's Sunday morning outing, I circled the aisle once more. After finding my couple of items, I walked up to the couple. "Hi, I couldn't help but notice your notebook and you discussing your items. Do you mind my asking you about this?"

The husband and wife lit up while the daughters listened with wide eyes and open ears.

"This is how I grew up, watching my parents shop with coupons, so I now shop with coupons." the husband said.

"I am so impressed with your amazing coupon notebook and how organized it seems." I said. "Also that you not only take the time to shop as a couple but as a family."

He thanked me and I turned to the girls.

"Girls, your parents are being a great example to you on how to save money and shop."

At the checkout, I said "I am so touched by what you are doing together and your example to your daughters. Do you mind if I ask, do you know how much money you save in a year by using coupons?"

The wife smiled proudly and said "we saved around $1000 last year."

Little did they know the impression they left on me beyond their savings. I walked out of CVS having been changed by a family whose names I don't know nor will probably ever see again. I was touched by this couple's ability to communicate tenderly over small decisions. If they could purchase the small things of life like makeup and shampoo together, I knew they were able to discuss larger purchases and issues.

Parents desire to model to their children important life lessons. Way beyond saving money, their grandparents and parents modeled what everyone really desires . . . togetherness and good communication. Whether through discussing money and savings or enjoying the simplest everyday task of shopping with someone, life is more pleasurable with others vs. doing it alone.

They say it is the little things in life that make a difference. The amount of money we spend on loved ones does not buy closeness or intimacy. Whether we spend pennies or pounds, it is how we communicate and connect with people that brings connection.

I walked away desirous of the tender interaction this couple and family had together. I took their example home with me to become a better team player with my husband over finances and with my children over simple, everyday experiences. I went home desirous simply to ask my husband and children to help me with common, everyday tasks and me to volunteer to help them with their tasks.

While I didn't sit in church with my husband and listen to a sermon that Sunday, somehow God orchestrated a pertinent and timely message for me in CVS. I'm thankful for the family I encountered that Sunday morning. Little did they know the huge imprint they left on me. I left CVS having saved 20% off my total purchase, along with a 100% bonus of valuable life lessons. The CVS Coupon Couple were a *blessing in disguise.*

Grace S. Johnson - A Touch of Grace - Interior Accessory Designer. Decorating expresses one side of Grace's creativity, while words express the other side of Grace's creative soul. She enjoys writing letters, poems, devotionals and stories to encourage others. Married 38 years, has twin daughters and a son.

# Crossroad Moments – Choosing Faith Over Fear

*Karen L. Wisniewski*

What happens at the crossroads when we put FAITH over fear? Esther was faced with a "Crossroads moment" when she was told: ". . . who knows but that you have come to a royal position for such a time as this" (Esther 4:14 NIV).

Basically, Mordecai was saying that God will have His way with or without her. The choice was hers: would she risk her life to go before the King? Would fear stop her? Or would she participate in God's great plan?

Esther, a Jewish woman, had been chosen out of many young ladies to be queen – an impossible feat!

Esther had learned of a secret plan by the second in command to the King to destroy the Jews – an impossible find!

Esther, though queen, had to enter the throne room uninvited – prepared for the worst (death), but hoping for the best (the king to extend his scepter) – an impossible situation!

Esther's God – our God – is the God of the impossible...

Esther fasted, prayed, and CHOSE to participate in God's plan. She traveled the narrow path that looked dark and bleak, and she could only see one step ahead. Her FAITH triumphed over her fear for she knew in her heart that she was alive for such a time as this.

And just like Esther, YOU are alive for such a time as this.

So when we come to our own "crossroads moment" in life (and we all have them) – it boils down to making a choice to participate in God's plan or not. In Jeremiah 6:16 we are told, "Stand at the crossroads and look, ask for the ancient path, ask where the good way is, and walk in it, and you will find rest for your souls. But you said, 'we will not walk in it.'"

Why would anyone *not* want to go the way God says is GOOD? After all, He tells us that he has plans to prosper us and to give us a hope and a future (Jeremiah 29:11)!

Could it be because we struggle to put FAITH over fear? If so, let's learn how to recognize the elements of fear that can contaminate our F.A.I.T.H.

1. Familiarity – The well-traveled road gives us what we expect. Even if there is discomfort on this path, it is less uncomfortable than the unknown . . . so Familiarity contaminates our faith.
2. Anxiety – FEAR (False Evidence Appearing Real) and anxiety come straight from the father of lies (Satan) and are some of his biggest tactics to stop us in our tracks. When we come to believe a lie as the truth it breeds anxiety…and Anxiety contaminates our faith.
3. I doubt – The enemy plants seeds of doubt, and we live in disbelief about having the abundant life God has promised us. We live with the inconsistency that rests between our belief and unbelief – can His promises be true for me? . . . so when I doubt, it contaminates my faith.
4. Too hard – God's way (the ancient way) looks too difficult. We don't know how to navigate the new journey before us. Despite the promised victory, we question our ability. We know we can't do it on our own and forget that all things are possible with God. We deem it too hard, and that contaminates our faith.

5. **H**alf-interested – Complacency creates a lukewarm faith. We become like the servant who buried his talents to keep them safe – he didn't try to grow what he had been given to glorify his master. When we go through the motions to maintain the status quo, we become complacent. Half-interested approaches contaminate our faith.

I believe that the real battle amid all of our emotions is to recognize that Satan is the one at work trying to contaminate our faith. He is trying to stop us at the crossroads.

But, God says, "Fear not, for I am with you; Be not dismayed, for I am your God. I will strengthen you. Yes, I will help you, I will uphold you with My righteous right hand." (Isaiah 41:10 NIV)

My question for you is this . . . Will you keep your FAITH pure so that nothing can stop you from stepping out for such a time as this?

My challenge to you is this . . . Give your best "YES!" to God. It is Possible!


Karen L. Wisniewski holds Jesus as her Lord, Savior, Redeemer and Guide. Her greatest joy is found in sharing her faith at every opportunity. As a Christian Life Coach, Karen is passionate about setting captives free so they can live their abundant life as followers of Christ as in John 10:10.

# A Journey Interrupted

*Juanita Copley*

I was totally frustrated and angry! My flight from Newark to Chicago O'Hare had just been canceled after being delayed and rescheduled for the fourth time, and I was already six hours late! I was on the fourth leg of a weeklong journey from Houston to the east coast to the mid-west and then home. I was so tired and frankly, sick of people! Most importantly, I had purposely scheduled a day with my daughter in Chicago when I arrived and now, I wasn't sure I could even get there!

After another hour had passed, I was assigned to "the last seat" on an airline I had never heard of Kiwi Airlines. I quickly prepared to board the plane and in the process, I made a silence covenant. I was not going to talk with anyone. If possible, I was going to sleep and do my best to calm down. When we finally boarded the plane at 10:00 pm, there were actually three available seats, all in the same row. How exciting! Thank you God! I certainly deserved the three seats. There was room for my bags and I could even stretch out! And then, it happened.

Just as we were getting ready to take off, the stewardess explained that we had one more passenger. I sighed, looked up and saw a beautiful, yet clearly distressed woman holding more bags than she should have on a plane and I knew my excitement was short-lived. She struggled to her window seat, moved my bags, hit me with one of hers, and then sat down. Immediately, she broke my silence covenant and asked me why I was going to Chicago. I responded that

I was going to see my daughter who was a student at college. When she asked where, I told her it was a small Christian university and she probably had never heard of it … Olivet Nazarene University. She said, "I know Nazarene. In fact, there was only one man that had ever made a positive difference in my life and that man was a Nazarene minister. I went to his church when I lived in Chicago." She then went on to say that her life was a total catastrophe. With tears streaming down her face, she explained that she had decided her life was just not worth living. In fact, she had just left her home and job in New Jersey and was going to see her family one last time. In her mind, life was over.

At that moment, my covenant of silence was over. I quietly said, "My dad was a Nazarene minister. He passed away a few years ago at age 56. In fact, he pastored Chicago First Church of the Nazarene for only 18 months many years ago. I asked who her pastor was and she replied, "Bill Varian." With tears now streaming down my face, I said, "That was MY Dad!" For the next four hours on a darkened, quiet plane, Jesus came and sat in the middle seat between two ladies . . . one from Houston and one from New Jersey who had a God-anointed appointment about a Pastor Father who lived in Chicago. In the presence of God Almighty, we talked, shared experiences, prayed, cried, and prayed some more. When we arrived and stood to leave the plane, a little lady in the row in front of us, turned around and said, "Hallelujah! God visited all of us tonight!" She was right. I have a feeling that many people on that plane heard our conversation that night. We parted as changed people. God interrupted our journey in an unexpected way and together we experienced the grace, mercy, and love of God.

I realize that my journey has been interrupted by unexpected events many times, some good and some bad. I am beginning to see that with God's grace and truth, I have experienced so much more good than I ever expected. I have journeyed . . .

- From the unfaithfulness of a spouse in a relationship and divorce to a beautiful marriage of 36 years to the love of my life;
- From poverty as a single mom to a life of unbelievable blessings, including money and so much more;
- From cancer, radiation and chemo for my husband and my 4-year-old grandson to an understanding of illness and hurts as well as the tender arms of a loving God and healer;
- From the death and loss of my beloved husband, my precious parents, and many close friends to an understanding of grief combined with new perspectives and yearnings for a heavenly home.

God's truth has helped me see my life journey through the eyes of an "eternal picture." Rather than dwelling on the events that I don't understand or attempting to help God see *my* plan, I think about my life as a continuous journey and how God's purposes can be accomplished through me with an eternal perspective. My favorite verses from Proverbs (with my amplified comments), remind me of God's grace and truth.

"Trust in the Lord with all thy heart." (He has never forgotten me!) "And lean not unto thine own understanding." (I have no doubts that my knowledge will not be enough to face the many experiences I have and will experience.) "In all thy ways acknowledge Him." (My Creator, the One who couldn't love me more or less no matter what I do!) "And He will direct your path." (Sometimes through silence sometimes through open or closed doors, sometimes with a direct Word, and yes, sometimes with an unexpected experience.)

I have learned so much during my "almost 70-year" journey. I continue to learn 1) I can choose my responses to life events, 2) I can depend on a God Incarnate who has created and understands me, and 3) God is in control of all things. His grace and truth are all I need for true joy and peace. Bring on those interruptions. God and I can handle them!


Juanita Copley has recently retired from a 48-year career teaching Prekindergarten to graduate students. Nita has traveled extensively both nationally and internationally and she would like to share her experiences with others, the truths that God has taught her, and the rich grace that He has provided throughout her life.

# Missed Bus

*Alicia Herrington*

The light is fading. It's not even 6 yet but dusk is almost over. The breeze is warm. You can't tell it's almost October.

Leaves don't seem to fall here, the climate is too warm. Too bad. I miss the colors of fall. The world fading around me.

Groceries bumping, bumping in the bags against my back. Hurry down the path. The fountain gurgles as I go past.

Vendors trying to get me to buy food. Ignore them.
I already ate. And besides, I still don't know what half this stuff is. Even if I did we don't speak the same language. Makes shopping hard.

Have to hurry now. I want to get home before it's too dark out. I'm not sure I'll recognize my stop in the dark.

Cross the street now. Move with the pack. Hand up and firm glare.
Don't even think about turning, buddy. It's my time to go. Wait your turn.

There's the bus stop. A bus is already there. 209. I think that's my bus. Have to run for it.
Run. Run. Got to make it. Just a little bit further. Just have to reach the door.

Drat. Didn't make it. Now I'm stuck waiting here. Sign says next bus 20 minutes.

No taxis in sight. Still don't have DiDi on my phone. No choice but to wait it out.

Earbuds in. Music on. Not like anyone is going to talk to me.
Not like I could understand them if they did.

Light keeps fading. Bus sign changes. Adds another five minutes.
It's full dark now. Why does it get dark so early here?
It's not even the end of September. It shouldn't look like midnight.

Still waiting. Been half an hour now. I'm not alone anymore. Lots of people here.
Every time we see a bus we all start to stand but it's never the right bus.

Finally. The right bus. Everybody standing up. The crowd moves as one.
Pushing, shoving, trying to get to the door. Trying to get a seat.

Elbow to ribs. Ow. Knocked into the guy beside me. I'm not good at this game.
One day I will be, but not yet.
Right now all is confusion, and chaos, and too many bodies in too little space.

I do not get a seat.

At least I am able to claim a spot to stand by the back door.
From there it is easier to see the stops. Easier to know when to get off.

I feel a breeze through the window. This is nice.
Makes it feel less crowded than it is.

It's a half an hour ride back to my stop. Longer if there's traffic.
I hope there's not traffic. Chinese traffic is terrifying.

First stop. People get off. No one gets on though.
Bus is headed the wrong direction for that.

Next stop. The park. Watch the dancing grannies go through their routine.
Slow movements, set to fast music.

Hospital next. No one off. No one on.
Moving on.

Now the restaurant with the broken fountain. It looks sad, all full of dirt and trash.
Especially with the neon restaurant lights behind it.

Moore stops. People off at each of them. Off to shops. Apartments. Home.
Wish I was one of them.

Finally. The basketball courts. Kids playing under the florescent light.
Only a few stops left now. Got to keep watch.

Getting darker. Not as many lights in this area. No neon.
Keep my eyes peeled. Don't want to miss the place.

Breeze ruffling my hair. Push it away.
Something in the sky. Stop! Look again. What's that?
That can't be right. More lights? Here? No. Oh. Stars.

There's really stars. They're really there.
I haven't seen the stars since I got here. It's too busy.

There's too much light. Too many people. Too much smog.

But there they are. Dancing above my head.

The wind continues to blow through the window.
Worship music starts playing through my earbuds.
The stars continue their chorus overhead.
"The heavens declare" my soul sings.

For this one moment I am not alone, on a bus, in a strange country.
For this one moment everything is perfect.

Then it's over. The bus pulls into the stop.
As soon as the doors open, I jump out.
You have to or they might close them on you.

Still the feeling of the moment remains.
That perfect moment of the feeling of dancing with the heavens, with nature, and with nature's God.

And as I walk back to my apartment, I'm so glad I missed the bus.

Alicia Herrington spent a year living in China (much to her mother's consternation). While there she traveled to many cities and took many buses. Despite being severely directionally challenged she almost never got lost. In her family's opinion this may be considered something of a miracle.

# A Son's Sacrifice – A Father's Redemption

*Dawn M. Durkee*

Harry and Florence Daly and their four boys lived on Eighth street, between Saint Augustine's Catholic Church and McCulligan's Pub, of which the family paid equal respect depending on the day of the week. The Daly boys went to Catholic grade school. The oldest son was my father, James. My grandmother made no bones about the fact that my father was her favorite. He was driven, responsible, a hard worker, and crazy smart.

The Daly's were a blue-collar family. They lived in Barberton at a time when the rubber factories were flourishing. My grandfather built tires for Seiberling Rubber. My father also worked at the factory, but as a foreman. He was an excellent critical thinker, a problem solver. He could keep his men working and the tires rolling.

My parents had three children. Scott was the oldest, then Greg. I was the baby girl. Scott was a driven, hard-working first-born son, like his father. He was also spontaneous, athletic, and spiritual. According to our father, life was based on facts and logic. Scott was full of determination and passion — when he set a course, nothing could stop him!

Dad's skills of management and arbitration would reach beyond the tire factory. He spent his days at Seiberling Rubber Factory, and his nights at Akron School of Law. He would graduate, build a private practice and eventually be elected as Ward Councilman, City Prosecutor, and finally Safety Director. Any hour Dad was not serving in one of these capacities, you could find him at a sporting event with one of his sons. They were the next generation of Daly men.

Scott's ambitions focused on the world of fitness, both personally and professionally. He quickly earned accolades body building and working for a major fitness enterprise. Scott's charisma and drive quickly led him to the top in his field. He believed in being healthy and he lived and looked the part. His charm and genuine compassion for others made him a huge success . . . and a lot of money.

Scott and Dad shared a deep admiration for one another. However, there was one topic that was not to be discussed – personal faith. Scott had an intimate relationship with his Savior and shared his faith spontaneously and fervently. "J-E-S-U-S" was embroidered with bright letters across the back of his jean jacket. James Daly, logical attorney, self-made man, would quickly put an end to any conversation spiritual in nature, even with his son. "Enough! That's okay for you! I just don't believe." Scott's heart ached that he could not share with his Dad the joy of a soul set free, and the hope of eternity.

One Sunday afternoon, the family got a call from my sister-in-law. "Scott and I are at the hospital. We thought it was strep throat, but the doctors have said to call the family." My husband, a paramedic, said, "We need to go quickly." Scott had contracted a virus, commonly called the "Flesh Eating Disease" which typically devours a victim's healthy cells within 24 hours. Scott fought five long, grueling days. He was the strongest person we had ever known, yet the virus enslaved him. Scott's wife continued to desperately plead at his bedside, "You can beat this babe! We are praying! You got this!" The doctor's assured us there was no hope. Our father with a heart of despair, yet mercy for his son, whispered in her ear, "You need to let him go. He is fighting so hard for you. Tell him you will be okay." Through a strength not her own, she relented, telling him she would see him again in glory. Scott breathed his last moments later. It was Good Friday.

Scott's services were held the following Monday at his church. There were more people than I had ever seen at a funeral. Scott was well-loved! According to those that spoke at his funeral, Scott was a benevolent man, a devout man of faith who lived that faith through his life choices. My father had missed out on this part of son. With grief and anguish in his eyes, he could not help but admit, "There was an undeniable Presence in that service."

It was not long after Scott's death that my father's own health began to fail. Greg and I were hopeful that the countless procedures and long hospitals stays would result in rehabilitation, but Dad's spirit was depleted. His heart was broken. Then Dad did something quite unexpected — he gave us permission to invite a certain preacher to come see him. This pastor knew my dad just from being a part of our small community and an occasional greeting at the local McDonald's. He knew a bit of our family history and my father's past resistance to faith. He felt honored that Dad would request his presence. He ultimately spent many hours at my father's side even though Dad had never entered the doors of his church. He and my father developed a mutual respect. At the time of my dad's passing, this pastor was engaged to speak at a conference in another state. When he received our call, he quickly boarded a plane to give my father's personal and powerful eulogy, of a broken man redeemed.

Am I implying that Scott was the sacrificial lamb for my father, that because of the unmistakable presence of the Holy Spirit at my brother's funeral that my stoic father was willing to consider the possibility of an Ultimate Being who not only governed the world, but knew his son on a personal and intimate level? Am I suggesting that my brother's death could have been orchestrated, or at least been permitted, by a Sovereign God for the sole purpose of bringing my father to the foot of the Cross? I am not only implying it, I am claiming it with all certainty! Was it not God who sacrificed His one and only Son for you and for me? The Sacrifice of a Son for the redemption of man. It's the Gospel.

Dawn M. Durkee is a wife, mother, grandmother, and social worker. She and her husband enjoy receiving guests in their century home in Canal Fulton, Ohio, offered on AirBnB. Dawn writes to glorify her Creator and Redeemer, and to encourage others, sharing personal moments gleaned on her journey with Christ.

# This is the Greatest Show

*Cindi Raymond*

*"We have this as a sure and steadfast anchor of the soul, a hope that enters into the inner place behind the curtain."*
~ Hebrews 6:19 (ESV)

Reading: Hebrews 6:9-20

The spectators file into the 20,000 seat, sold-out arena while palpable waves of anticipation ebb and flow through the gathering crowd. Applause grows — the main act is near. Heightened expectations crescendo and then, the spotlight stops center stage as the curtains float open. There he is waiting . . . Hugh Jackman: The Greatest Showman!
My friends and I have memorized the soundtrack. We know exactly what to expect...or do we? Instead of the diatribe of musical ensembles, this showman's story captivated me as he told of his journey to destinations he never thought possible. "That's me!" I shouted silently as my mind wandered back to July 4, 1976 . . .
America is 200 years old and I am eight! Friends and family are gathered to celebrate. The smell of charcoal, burgers, and the lake waft amongst laughter and play. Running; jumping; squealing with delight. Then, I hear it, "Too much, Cindi!" It is a phrase I would often hear as a child. Too loud. Too late. Too rambunctious. Too much. The youngest of six children by nine years made for a special blend of love, encouragement and yes, frustration.

My mind swirls with contradictions of thought. I am too much. I am too little. I am never enough. What one sees as strength; others judge as weakness. What is the truth? What is the lie? Do I believe falsehoods instead of truth? Am I believing as truth that which is a lie? For what am I destined?

But, God! That is the message I heard in my spirit as I watched The Greatest Showman. God uses His promises during seasons of doubt to remind us of truth.

In John 17:17, Jesus prays, *"Sanctify them in the truth; your word is truth."* As God's story unfolds, we come to understand that God's Word is not just true — it is truth itself. It is the standard by which every proclamation of truthfulness may be measured. Because of this, we read Hebrews 6:9-11 knowing that we are His beloved. He says we are enough. God is just; our salvation is secure.

This God-inspired writing to Jewish Christians is encouragement to hold fast amid doubt.

These early believers were tempted to abandon their faith in God, but hope was refreshed despite hardship and discouragement. They recalled the example of Abraham's patient endurance. And though, he did not see his innumerable descendants, he did see God's truth revealed at the birth of Isaac. God did not fail Abraham – He did not fail the Jewish Christians. Likewise, He does not fail us.

Believers are called to heed these examples of enduring faith as blessings despite the perception or reality of our circumstance. Hebrews 6:18 confirms for us, *". . . that by two unchangeable things, in which it is impossible for God to lie, we who have fled for refuge might have strong encouragement to hold fast to the hope set before us."*

Did you hear that? God does not lie! Truly, we are challenged to look beyond our disappointments; our inability, and beyond the lie that we are not enough. We are dared to trust in the hope that points to His redeeming love.

He knows truth because He is truth. He has written our story for His glory. Though we are rocked by troubled waters; though the journey may look different than we imagined, we need not be adrift with doubt. We are anchored on the Rock. (Hebrews 6: 19-20)

While Hugh Jackman may be regarded as the greatest showman, Jesus is the greatest show! He has gone before, drawn back the curtain, and is the true treasure!

So, yes. Sometimes I am too much. Sometimes I am too little. But with God, I am enough. So, I pray that today will be the day that you, too, trust in this precious treasure. Let today be the day that you stand on stage with the word of your testimony declaring that despite bitter times, Jesus promises the truth of a better way.

**Prayer:** Dear God, I believe you are the Almighty Creator that anchors my soul. Forgive me when I allow the bitterness of self-condemnation to grow in my heart because of misplaced doubt. Thank you for the certainty of your promises. Today, help me choose the better way of your truth that I may know you more intimately, love you more deeply, and serve you with purpose. In Jesus' name, amen.

**Reflect:** What are some things you doubt despite knowing God's truth? How does the truth of God's promises dispel those lies and confirm that you are enough?

Cindi Raymond is a follower of Jesus Christ, wife, mother, grandmother, and nationally known speaker with a heart for women to know God intimately, love Him deeply and serve Him on purpose. With Proverbs 20:5 as her life mission, she encourages generations of women to acknowledge and fulfill their anointing.

# Blessings
## COUNT THEM ONE BY ONE

# Serendipity and Me!

*Carol E. Veenstra*

The word serendipity became a part of my life as I entered retirement and began musing about years past. As life unfolded in my mind I began to see God's engineering that can only be described as serendipitous: delightful, totally unexpected events.

As a girl I had the desire to become a nurse, however, there were twists and turns on the road to writing RN after my name. The first turn appeared as I approached high school. I noticed a bump on my back and rushed to mom. We invested three years visiting doctors, learning about scoliosis and praying. I wondered how this flaw might impact becoming a nurse. In spite of my questions, I stayed involved in the future nurses club in high school, and continued taking college prep classes. As a senior the application process for nursing school became a priority, and a blanket of prayer covered every page.

I was learning about Jesus and His love for me during those years. He became my best friend. Nursing school and my back were at the top of my prayer list. My back turned out not to be a problem, and my dream of becoming a nurse was in view. Unbeknownst to me another life changing event was imminent.

The Sunday after my high school graduation I received a phone call from the Youth For Christ (YFC) Club Director in my city. I had seen him many times during YFC events however, conversation was incidental. That afternoon he asked if I would go with him to the YFC Singspiration that evening! Huh – that was unexpected! I said, "okay"

Preparing for nursing school and non-stop dating with Paul gobbled up every moment that spring and summer. Then Paul accepted a job as Director of YFC in Schenectady, New York. He moved over 500 miles away as I went to live at the convent called nursing school where students were not allowed to marry.

As my nursing career progressed I found myself in patients' homes teaching new moms about caring for babies, and learning there are endless horizons to pursue teaching about disease management and prevention. I thought, "What a wonderful thing to help prevent illness in addition to coming to the rescue after an assault on health had already occurred." My interest in community health took root (Jeremiah 29:11).

For the next two years Paul and I kept the US postal Service busy: no internet or texting available in those days. During one of his visits back to Michigan he presented me with a diamond ring and asked if I would marry him. I accepted his sweet proposal, and a new track was established in my whirring brain unaware that God's serendipity was cascading all around me. During that year we talked about getting married in the next fall. I would switch back to my pursuit of nursing somewhere down the road.

After months of planning we were married and settled in Schenectady. Over the next four years we welcomed two delightful children into our new family, Bonnie and Andy. Paul and I agreed I would be a stay-at-home-mom. We worked at pouring the love of Jesus into two young lives. Singing, *Jesus Loves Me* and *Jesus Loves the Little Children* was heard often in our home whether we were changing diapers, feeding or playing. We were blessed! We had two delightful babies and Jesus became our Mentor for parenting.

Years passed and Bonnie and Andy were well established in school. We had moved to Grand Rapids Michigan where I jumped back on my dream path and enrolled in the community college. While Andy and Bonnie went to school, so did I. I graduated, passed the licensing exam and wrote RN after my name!

I had a conference with Abba, my heavenly Father, for guidance looking for a job. The first response to my prayer came from a community hospital. This was not my first choice, but I accepted it not wanting to miss an opportunity. I was hired as a charge nurse with an array of opportunities to expand my skills (Romans 8:14-17).

As I worked at the hospital I was awakened to the fact that this hospital was a part of the county health system, which included the visiting nurses, providing in-home care, and preventive care through clinics, school nursing and many other services throughout our community. I became excited and nervous. "Dare I ask for a transfer to the health department with only a two year degree? What did I have to lose?" To my delight I was hired, and my passion to prevent, not just treat the hurts of life, popped to the surface, as another huge, serendipitous, surprise!

It had to be a miracle that Abba had planned long ago: before I left nursing school, before my struggles about my back, and, yes, before I was born, He had this very special, orchestrated, blessing in disguise planned for His little girl (Psalm 139:13-16). His purposes and my desires had merged! The twists and turns along the way were all integral to my Father's plan including community health nursing that has fit in with kids camps and short term mission trips scattered along life's way.

The adventure persists as God continues to sprinkle delightful surprises, which are welcomed with expectation and the realization of His awesome serendipity.

References: Jeremiah 29:11, Romans 8:14-17, Psalm 139:13-16

My careers have taken me through raising two wonderful children and being a community health nurse for 20+ years. God has given me the privilege of serving on several short-term mission teams with Paul to Puerto Rico, Eastern Europe, Central Asia and Southeast Asia. We have also invested time in various Bible camp ministries through the years.

# Expectations with Elizabeth and Mary

*Phyllis Wynsma*

Christmas is coming for us, and it was coming for Elizabeth and Mary as well. It was just around the corner. However, Elizabeth and Mary didn't know it, because for them, it was just winter and more winter; "Always winter but never Christmas" as C.S. Lewis writes in his Narnia book series.

And so it happened that for three long winter months, Elizabeth and Mary reflected on the events that brought them together and began to change their lives.

It all started with an angel named Gabriel. Mary probably told Elizabeth how unexpectedly this angel fluttered into her life with those words: "Greetings, you are highly favored! The Lord is with you." (Evidently angels don't generally make appointments before visiting, as a commentator puts it, and goes on to say: It was as if Mary was being congratulated for winning the grand prize in a contest she had never entered!)

Mary went on to tell Elizabeth that she was troubled by the Angel's words, but then Gabriel had told her not to be afraid because she had found favor with God. He had said, "You will be with child and you will give birth to a son, and you are to give him the name of Jesus. He will be great and will be called the Son of the Most High. The Lord will give him the throne of his father David and he will reign over the house of Jacob forever. His kingdom will never end."

So Mary continued her conversation, "I didn't see how this could be, since I was a virgin." But then Gabriel responded with these words: "The Holy Spirit will come upon you.... and by the way your older cousin Elizabeth is now in her seventh month of pregnancy, for nothing is impossible with God." (Luke 1:26-36). So Mary told the Angel, "I am the Lord's servant; may it be to me as you have said, and may everything you said come true."

Mary was thrilled to be at her cousin Elizabeth's house for a while. It had been a long, tiring trip from Nazareth (64 miles) to her small town near Jerusalem. It was good to be with family and share what she had experienced back in Nazareth with that angel.

It was a wonderful winter break for Elizabeth as well as she welcomed Mary to her home. Elizabeth was a small town girl who was married to Zacharias, a priest.

According to Leviticus law, a priest could marry any woman whose moral behavior was totally blameless. Elizabeth was this upright person.

So, it was with great excitement that Elizabeth said: " The same angel, Gabriel, that you encountered also paid a visit to Zacharias while he was burning incense in the temple some time ago." He told my husband, "Don't be afraid! Your prayers have been answered. Your wife will bear you a son and you shall call him John." Elizabeth continued, "It was at this point that Zacharias questioned Gabriel far too strongly and Gabriel caused Zacharias to be without speech for months." (Luke 1:19,20)

Oh boy! New life was about to enter Elizabeth's quiet house but for now the mothers-to-be waited out their pregnancies. So the mother of John, the preparer of the way, and the mother of the Messiah, whose way must be prepared were in conversation. Elizabeth acknowledged Mary as the mother of the Lord, "Blessed among women". As they spoke, Elizabeth's baby leaped in her womb as if to welcome the baby in Mary's womb. (Luke 1:41)

They must have laughed and talked a lot. We can imagine their expectations, but what about their conversations? Both knew God through the Books of Moses, the Psalms and the writings of the prophets of the Old Testament. They must have marveled at Micah the prophet's prediction of Jesus birth in Bethlehem, hundreds of years before Jesus birth. (Micah 5:2) Or perhaps Isaiah 9:6 with more prophecies: "For unto us a child is born, unto us a Son is given." Then Isaiah 7:14, "A virgin will be with child."

Well, time was passing and Mary had to return to Nazareth to prepare for the trip to Bethlehem. It was during those days that Caesar Augustus issued a decree that a census should be taken for registration and tax collection. So Joseph and Mary both needed to register in Bethlehem because both belonged to the house and line of David. (Luke 2:4,5)

Meanwhile, back in Jerusalem, the time had come for John the Baptist to be born. The neighbors and relatives of Elizabeth shared her joy and new expectations broke loose. A new future was dawning for the entire Jewish nation. People began to look forward to what God was going to do. They were prepared for great things to come through John, the preparer of the way, and for Jesus the Messiah.

Back in Bethlehem, the registration took a lot of time for Joseph and Mary. The city was full of people, as they expected, because Bethlehem was situated on the caravan route from Jerusalem to Hebron.

So the inns were all full, but a stable was prepared for their newborn son. That night a bright star appeared and an army of angels sang to proclaim the birth of the Savior of the world.

We can't help but wonder if Gabriel was in that angelic choir, for the Scriptures say, "Suddenly a great company of the heavenly hosts appeared with the angel praising God and saying, Glory to God in the highest and on earth, peace, good will to men." (Luke 2: 13, 14)

Phyllis Wynsma teaches Bible Study classes to women of all ages in various churches and communities. Phyllis is married, has three children, several grandchildren and great grandchildren. She shares her time between Michigan and Florida.

# He Stayed On the Cross

*Kimberly J. Price*

He stayed on the cross
And did not come down,
He could've called 10,000 angels
But instead, he made no sound.

They didn't have to drag him
Or force him to take that walk,
On the way to Golgotha
On the way to the cross.

This is why he came
His final act of love,
Laying down his life,
To secure heaven above.

They did not take his life
He freely gave it up for me,
He stayed on the cross
And died on that tree.

He knew this is what he had to do,
From the beginning of time
For it was God's plan,
Redemption was his design.

He stayed on the cross
And did not come down,
Until it was accomplished,
Until he won the crown.

Kimberly J. Price is a wife, mother, grandmother. Kimberly put writing on the back burner so that she could focus on raising her six children and be a full-time homemaker. Kimberly's life has had its share of struggles and its during those times that she's most inspired to pen a poem.

# The Asia Experiment

*Tracy Herrington*

Jolted awake by the sound of the land line ringing, I sat straight up in bed. It was 3:45 in the morning. No good call ever comes at that time. My husband had answered the phone. As he paced the bedroom floor, I knew my oldest daughter, the one who gives me gray hair, was on the other end of the line. Alicia was in China. It was 3:45 in the afternoon there.

Six weeks prior we had stood in Detroit Metro Airport and watched this adventure loving, directionally challenged, genius girl embark on a new quest. She had taken a position as a librarian at an international school in Suzhou. Letting her go (even at 26-years-old) had been gut-wrenching. She knew no one. She didn't speak the language, and common sense is not exactly her strength!

The morning she left was devastating for me. I had come to the place where I was confident that China was where God wanted her. But I wanted to grab hold of her with every fiber of my being and not let go. God had given me verses from I Corinthians that I was praying for her. *"For we don't want you to be unaware, brothers, of our affliction that took place in the province of Asia: we were completely overwhelmed – beyond our strength – so that we even despaired of life. However, we personally had a death sentence within ourselves so that we would not trust in ourselves, but in God who raises the dead"* (2 Corinthians 1:8-9, HCSB).

Okay, I understand that the area they were referring to as Asia is not how we think of it today, but the verses were written just for my girl, or so I thought. The morning she was leaving, I answered a call from my neighbor of 20 years, Leah.

"Did you get the gift I left by your front door last night?" she asked.

"We did, but I haven't opened it yet," I responded. "I'm waiting for Alicia to get out of the shower. Then we'll open it together."

"Oh. I was hoping that you opened it last night. So, you haven't read the card yet?"

Leah was a flight attendant whose normal itinerary included the Detroit to Shanghai route. She hadn't been scheduled for my daughter's flight but had begged co-workers to trade with her so that she could be on Alicia's plane. After no luck for weeks, a few days before, someone had finally agreed. At the time, I considered it a sign from God that my precious daughter would be looked after. Leah would ensure that Alicia would make her connection with the school representative that would meet her at the airport. (I had images from the movie "Taken" etched in my mind.)

"I'm so sorry, Tracy, but I had to back out of the flight. We have a family emergency. I need to leave this morning to go out of state."

Her words were like a punch in the gut. I mumbled my words of understanding and got off the phone before I totally broke down. I looked at my open Bible before me. The words I had been praying for Alicia blurred before my eyes. I had wanted her to know that when she was completely overwhelmed and couldn't trust her own ability, that God, who raises the dead, was and is trustworthy.

"Who needs to learn this?" I felt God gently say.

When I was completely overwhelmed, beyond my ability to endure, I put my trust in . . . my neighbor! Not God! As I prayed now, I gave my girl to God.

Now, six weeks later, Alicia was calling in the middle of the night. It was the first school vacation. She was living in the housing at the school, but the building was closing for ten days for the break. Her plan was to travel across China by herself with the Google translate app as her only form of communication. (Remember, I said common sense was not her strength?) She had taken the public transit bus to the train station. From there she was to go on to the airport and fly to Chengdu to see the famous pandas and on to Tibet. However, she had missed her train and was in danger of missing her flight. She couldn't read the signs, her translation app was down, and she didn't know what to do. She called home to ask us to pray for her. She was overwhelmed and was experimenting to see if God was trustworthy. We prayed. Being halfway around the world, it was all we could do and all we needed to do.

As soon as Alicia hung up the phone, a Chinese-American couple approached her. They had overheard her conversation. They spoke both English and Mandarin. Directing her to the appropriate line, this couple explained to her how to get re-ticketed for another train. I believe these people could have been angels. They were in my eyes!

This was the first of many times in the year that she was in China that we experienced God's faithfulness. A canceled flight by my neighbor and a missed train were the tools God used to teach both of us about God's character.

Tracy Herrington is the mom of three incredible girls and one amazing son-in-law. All of them occasionally give her gray hair and always keep her prayer life active. Having raised her daughters in the green-house of homeschooling, she is now watching the older two fly off to new adventures.

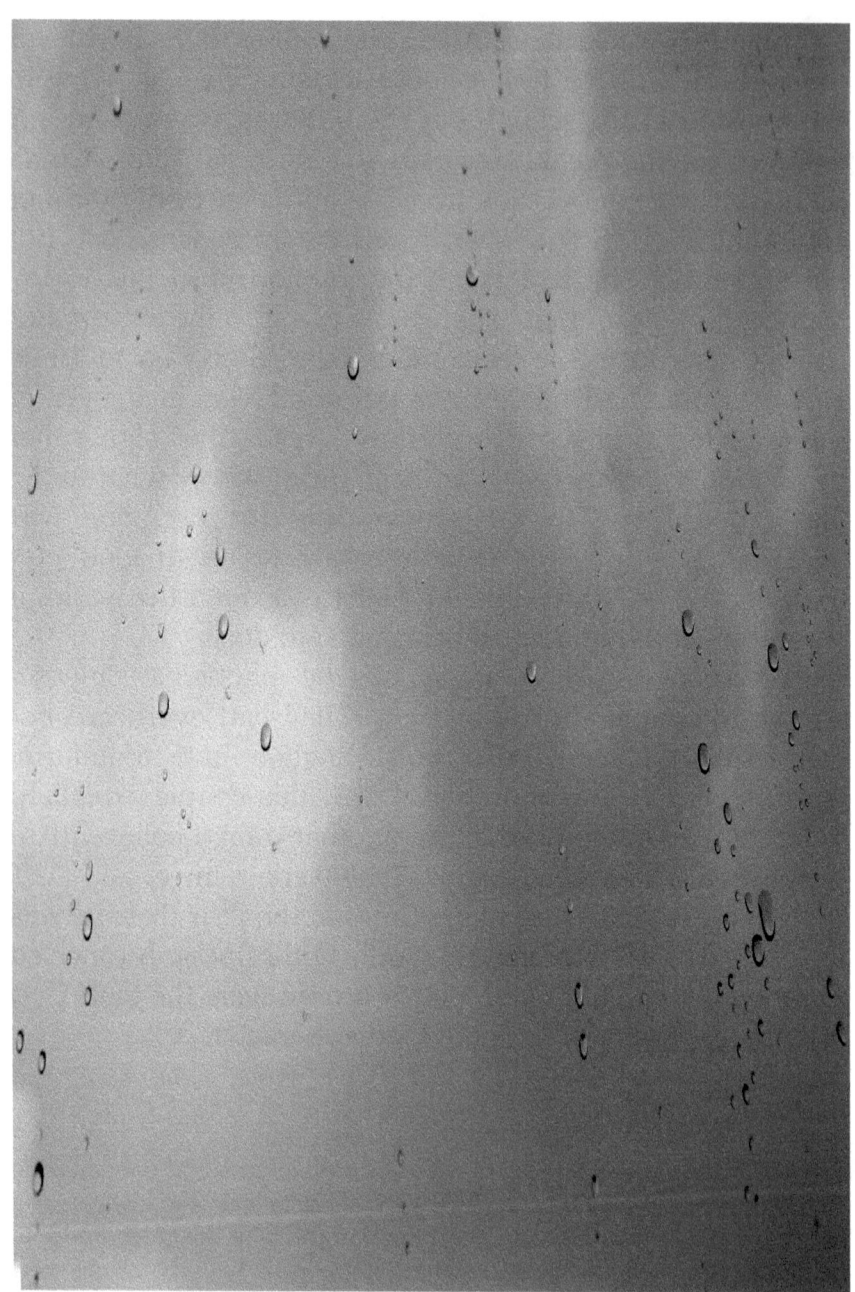

Living Parables of Central Florida, Inc., of which EABooks Publishing is a division, supports Christian charities providing for the needs of their communities and are encouraged to join hands and hearts with like-minded charities to better meet unmet needs in their communities. Annually the Board of Directors chooses the recipients of seed money to facilitate the beginning stages of these charitable activities.

## Mission Statement

To empower start up, nonprofit organizations financially, spiritually, and with sound business knowledge to participate successfully as a responsible 501(c)3 organization that contributes to the Kingdom work of God.

## Incubator Program

The goal of the Incubator Program: The Small Non-Profit Success Incubator Program, provides a solid foundation for running a successful non-profit through a year-long coaching process, eventually allowing these charities to successfully apply for grants and loans from others so they can further meet unmet needs in their communities.

Living Parables of Central Florida, a 501c3

www.ingramcontent.com/pod-product-compliance
Lightning Source LLC
Chambersburg PA
CBHW072035060426
42449CB00010BA/2267